MONSTERS

FRANKENSTEIN

BY ADAM WOOG

KIDHAVEN PRESS

An imprint of Thomson Gale, a part of The Thomson Corporation

THOMSON

™

GALE

Detroit • New York • San Francisco • San Diego
New Haven, Conn. • Waterville, Maine • London • Munich

LIBRARY OF CONGRESS CATALOGING-IN-PUBLICATION DATA

Woog, Adam, 1953–
    Frankenstein / by Adam Woog.
        p. cm. — (Monsters)
    Includes bibliographical references and index.
    ISBN 0-7377-3164-8 (alk. paper)
    1. Shelley, Mary Wollstonecraft, 1797-1851. Frankenstein—Juvenile literature.
    2. Frankenstein films—History and criticism—Juvenile literature. 3. Franken-
stein (Fictitious character)—Juvenile literature. 4. Monsters in literature—
Juvenile literature. I. Title. II. Monsters series (KidHaven Press)
    PR5397.F73W66 2006
    791.43'651—dc22
 	
                                                                            2005014644

Printed in China

CONTENTS

CHAPTER 1

"IT'S ALIVE!"

Frankenstein's monster may be the most famous creature in the world. This terrifying thing is almost human, but not quite. A scientist created him from the spare parts of dead people and then gave him life!

When most people think about Frankenstein's monster, they think about his most famous appearance, in a movie made in 1931. This movie, *Frankenstein*, made the monster a familiar figure. Many fans think the film is one of the best horror movies ever made. It is still a beloved story, even though it does not seem very scary compared to other movies.

In this movie, the monster is about 7 feet (2m) tall, with broad shoulders and long, strong arms and legs.

4

Frankenstein's monster is a hideous creature made from body parts taken from dead people.

Mary Wollstonecraft Shelley was only nineteen years old when she dreamed up the Frankenstein story.

His face is gray, and his cheeks look hollow. He has a square head, a high forehead, and deep-set eyes. Big electrical bolts stick out of his neck. The creature also has many scars—including one where the top of his head was removed so that he could get a new brain!

The monster wears black clothes that are ragged and too small. He has heavy boots and a clumsy way of moving, like a child who is just learning to walk. Also like a child, he enjoys simple things, such as the warmth of sunlight. However, the monster is **mute**. That means he cannot speak. He can only groan and grunt.

Knowing what to call this monster can be confusing. In the original story, the monster's creator is named Dr. Frankenstein. Over the years, however, the creature itself has come to be known as Frankenstein or Frankenstein's monster or, more simply, the monster.

A Monster Is Born

Whatever he is called, the monster was scaring people long before he became a movie star. The Frankenstein story began in 1816. That year, a nineteen-year-old English woman, Mary Wollstonecraft Shelley, was vacationing in Switzerland with friends, including two famous poets, Lord Byron and Percy Shelley.

The weather was bad, and the group had to stay indoors most of the time. To pass the time, they took turns writing ghost or horror stories and telling them to each other. Mary's contribution was inspired by a dream. It was about Dr. Victor Frankenstein, a scientist obsessed with finding the key to life. Dr. Frankenstein hopes that being able to create life will help him put an end to disease and death.

The scientist uses body parts from dead people to build a living creature. This monster is smart and sensitive, but he is also horribly ugly. Terrified, Dr. Frankenstein rejects his creation. The creature disgusts and scares everyone else as well. Lonely and suffering, the monster becomes a violent killer and then flees.

In this scene from the 1931 movie, Dr. Frankenstein and his assistant dig up dead bodies in a graveyard.

THE WRONG BRAIN!

Mary Shelley's story was a big hit when it was published in 1818. Over the next years, many plays, as well as a silent movie, were based on it. The details of the story changed often. The 1931 movie was also based only very loosely on the original story. However, it is the story that most people know today.

In this version, Dr. Frankenstein has a laboratory in a remote mountain region. He is secretly collecting dead bodies, hoping to use them to create a man. He and his assistant, Fritz, steal the bodies from graveyards and execution sites.

However, when they are nearly done with their task, Fritz makes a terrible mistake. He steals a brain from a medical college but accidentally drops a glass jar containing a healthy brain. He takes another

brain, even though it is labeled "**abnormal**." He has stolen the brain of a criminal!

"IT'S ALIVE!"

Meanwhile, Dr. Frankenstein's **fiancée**, Elizabeth, visits the scientist in his remote laboratory. Frankenstein's best friend, Victor, and his former professor, Dr. Waldman, go with her. They arrive just as Dr. Frankenstein is conducting his final experiment.

Using electricity from a crashing thunderstorm, Dr. Frankenstein gives his creature enough energy to live. Excitedly he shouts: "It's alive!" But in giving his creature life, Dr. Frankenstein realizes that he has made a terrible mistake. The monster's ugliness and strength frighten him, and the creature cannot be controlled.

Dr. Frankenstein tells a visitor to his laboratory about the monster lying on the table beneath a sheet.

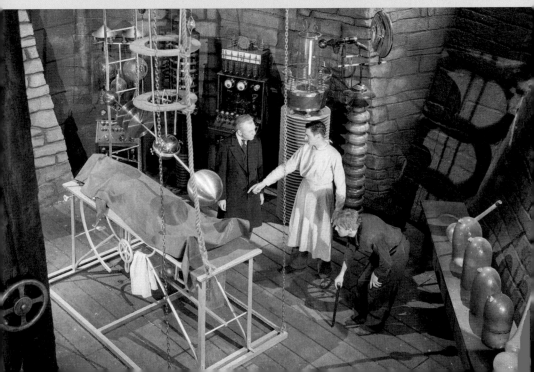

Dr. Frankenstein and Fritz lock the monster in a dark cellar. When Fritz cruelly abuses the monster, the creature fights back. He attacks and kills Fritz.

The months of hard work and bitter disappointment cause Dr. Frankenstein to collapse. He abandons his laboratory, going to his father's house to rest and prepare for his wedding to Elizabeth. Dr. Waldman stays behind to destroy the monster. However, the creature kills Dr. Waldman and then escapes into the mountains.

THE END OF THE MONSTER

While wandering in the mountains, the monster meets a young girl named Maria. Like a little child, the creature plays happily with her. However, he accidentally kills the girl. When they are throwing flowers into a lake to watch them float, the monster throws Maria in. He thinks that she will float, too, but she drowns instead.

The monster picks flowers by a lake with the young Maria.

The monster strangles Dr. Frankenstein as an angry mob watches in this scene from the movie's exciting ending.

Confused and upset, the monster wanders away. He finds the house where Dr. Frankenstein's wedding is about to occur. The creature confronts Elizabeth, but her terrified screams frighten him away. Meanwhile, Maria's father arrives in the village, sadly carrying his dead daughter.

The people of the town think that the monster killed Maria on purpose. An angry mob, including Dr. Frankenstein, heads out to find and destroy the creature. The mob has clubs, torches, and dogs.

In the mountains, the doctor and his creation have a face off. The monster overpowers Dr. Frankenstein, carries him to the top of an old windmill, and throws him out the window. Luckily, a blade of the mill breaks Dr. Frankenstein's fall and he survives. The mob then sets the windmill on fire around the tormented monster. As the movie ends, there is a brief scene in the home of Dr. Frankenstein's father.

The scientist is recovering from his wounds and plans to finally marry Elizabeth.

A Big Hit

The movie caused a scandal when it opened in 1931. People were really terrified! Because it was so shocking, some communities insisted that the movie be **censored**.

In England, for instance, three scenes were removed: when Frankenstein discovers Fritz's body, when Dr. Waldman is killed, and when the monster threatens Elizabeth. In Kansas, so many cuts were made that the film was about four minutes shorter. In Rhode Island, some newspapers refused to run ads for *Frankenstein* because it was so shocking. One observer commented, "The film has been imitated so much that today [it does not] bother people. But in 1931, it was awfully strong stuff."[1]

Despite the objections of the censors, *Frankenstein* was a big hit. Most movie critics loved it. For example, the *New York Times* named it one of the best films of the year. *Frankenstein* was also popular with audiences. Long lines formed at every theater. It quickly earned many times more than it had cost to make.

This success was a big surprise to the movie's makers. No one had guessed that *Frankenstein* would be a smash hit. They were simply trying to make a scary film, and they worked hard to do it well.

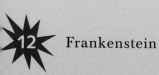

Chapter 2

The Making of Frankenstein

When *Frankenstein* was made in 1931, movies were still quite new. Many things that are standard today for moviemakers were not yet perfected. For example, movies had only had sound for a few years. (Before that, all films were silent.) Ways of creating special effects, makeup, and lighting were also crude by today's standards. Nonetheless, the movies were an exciting and popular form of entertainment.

In 1931 horror movies were becoming especially popular. Universal Studios, a Hollywood studio, was becoming known as a top producer of these films. It had recently scored a hit with *Dracula*. Many more horror movies would come, including *The Mummy* and *The Wolf Man*. Meanwhile, Universal wanted to follow *Dracula's* success with a version of the Frankenstein story.

ACTORS AND WRITERS

Frankenstein's producer was Carl Laemmle, Jr., the son of Universal's founder. Its director was James Whale, a talented Englishman. Together they chose the actors. Among them were Colin Clive, who played Dr. Frankenstein, and Mae Clarke, who played Elizabeth. For the important role of the monster, they picked an unknown English actor, William Henry Pratt. No one knew Pratt by that name, though; his **stage name** was Boris Karloff.

Englishman James Whale directed the 1931 Frankenstein *film.*

The tall, serious-looking Karloff joined the cast only after the producer and director had considered Bela Lugosi. Lugosi, the star of *Dracula*, turned down the part because it had no speaking lines. When Karloff got the role, Lugosi (who was then much better known) told him, "The part's nothing, but perhaps it will make you a little money."[2] It made Karloff world famous!

Two writers, Garrett Fort and Francis Faragoh, created the story for the movie. They changed many of the original novel's details. For example, they changed Dr. Frankenstein's first name from Victor to Henry. They also dropped many parts of Mary Shelley's story.

Probably the most important change the writers made was in the monster's character. In Shelley's novel, he is intelligent and thoughtful. He teaches himself to read and communicate. In addition, although he is violent, the monster also often has tender emotions.

Boris Karloff, dressed in his monster costume, takes a break with Colin Clive, the actor playing Dr. Frankenstein, during filming of the movie.

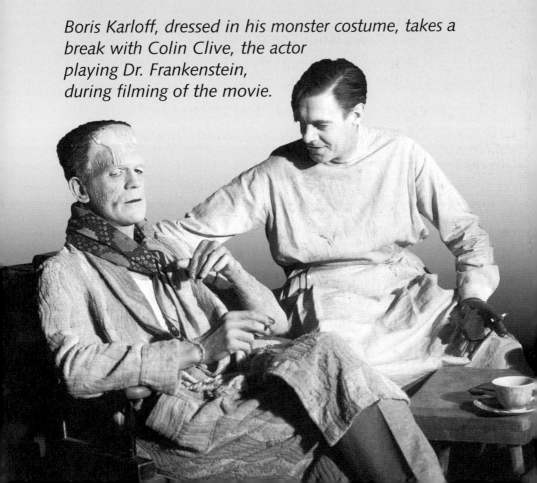

In the movie, the monster is less than human. The movie's writers gave the creature a criminal's brain, with only limited intelligence and emotions. He could sometimes be gentle, but mostly he was just angry, violent, and confused. In other words, he became a real monster.

MAKING A MONSTER

As the writers finished the screenplay, the moviemakers worked on other parts of the project. For example, they had to decide on the look of the monster. Jack Pierce, Universal's chief makeup artist, was the monster's main designer. He tried many different looks and made hundreds of sketches and models. He also spent four months researching subjects such as **surgery** and **anatomy**.

These studies helped Pierce create his design. For instance, he learned that there were many possible ways to cut a human skull and insert a brain. He decided that Dr. Frankenstein would choose the simplest way: cutting off the top, adding a hinge, and clamping it shut. This part of Pierce's design was even written into the script: "The top of its head has a curious flat ridge like the lid of a box. The hair is fairly short and quite obviously combed over the ridge to hide the [scar] where the brain was put in."[3]

Creating the makeup was as complicated as designing it. Pierce painted Karloff's face blue-green (so it looked gray in black-and-white film). He blackened the actor's fingernails with shoe polish and glued fake

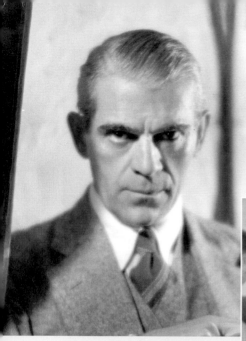

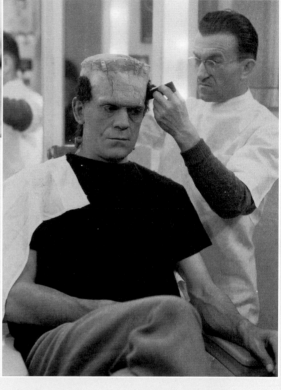

A makeup artist begins to transform Boris Karloff (left) into the monster.

electrical bolts to his neck. He fixed wire clamps over Karloff's lips and put wax on his eyelids to make his eyes seem dull. To make his cheeks seem hollow, Karloff removed his own partial false teeth.

Making the monster's costume was also complicated. Karloff's suit was made too small so that his arms and legs would look especially long. His boots weighed 13 pounds (6kg) each, and beneath his clothes the actor wore metal braces on his back and legs. These boots and braces were so heavy that Karloff had to lurch around like a baby just learning to walk.

Wearing his heavy costume and layers of make-up, Boris Karloff sits down to a meal on the movie set.

In costume, the actor was over 7 feet (2m) tall and weighed nearly 50 pounds (23kg) more than usual. At first, he spent six hours every day getting into his makeup and costume. (By the end of the **shooting schedule**, this took only about three

hours.) It took another two hours to get out of costume, so Karloff was working fifteen or more hours a day during the shoot!

SUFFERING ON THE SET

Being Frankenstein's monster was not just time-consuming, it was also painful and uncomfortable. The wax on Karloff's eyelids melted and hurt his eyes. The long underwear beneath his suit, which he wore to make himself bulky, was always wet with sweat. He seriously hurt his back because of the heavy back and leg braces and because he did most of his own stunts. Karloff actually lost 20 pounds (9kg) while filming.

Furthermore, the actor was forced to wear a veil over his face in public. This blinded him, so he had to be led by the hand to and from his dressing room. Laemmle ordered the veil after a studio secretary fainted when she saw Karloff in costume. Laemmle said the veil was a safety measure to protect other Universal employees from shock. Of course, news about it was also great advertising for Universal's upcoming movie.

Despite all the discomfort, Karloff was polite and good-humored throughout his ordeal. He said he was simply grateful to have the work. Besides, he did not suffer all the time. Whale made sure that the big actor had plenty of breaks in between scenes. The movie crew was always amused to see a fearful monster relaxing on the set with a cup of tea!

LIGHTS! CAMERA! SPECIAL EFFECTS!

Just as important as makeup to the movie's success was the film's spooky look. Whale worked hard to perfect this. He was helped by many others, including special-effects chief Ken Strickfaden and cameraman Arthur Edeson.

Some of *Frankenstein's* visual effects were achieved with dramatic lighting. For example, characters often first appear in darkness and then emerge suddenly into light. Also, Whale used Karloff's eerie stare to good effect. Furthermore, the director was inventive in building suspense with sound effects, such as the thunder and electrical noises of the storm scene.

The set design also helped give the movie a creepy look. For example, Dr. Frankenstein's laboratory looks like something from a nightmare. Its huge walls and stairs are strangely shaped, and the actors (especially Fritz and the monster) cast eerie shadows on them. The lab is also full of weird machines, electrical devices, and bubbling test tubes. In other words, it is a classic mad scientist's lab!

The most dramatic of the movie's special effects came during the electrical storm, when lightning gives power to the monster. *Frankenstein's* effects seem simple compared to movies today, but they were amazing for their time. They were so unusual that people from everywhere on the Universal lot came to watch them being filmed.

Test tubes bubble with strange liquids and giant machines operate as Dr. Frankenstein and his assistants work in the laboratory.

The hard work that went into the making of *Frankenstein* created an entertaining and scary movie. *Frankenstein* is more than that, however. It also asks serious questions about science and society.

CHAPTER 3

FRANKENSTEIN AND SCIENCE

Shelley's story about Dr. Frankenstein has been popular for nearly 200 years, mostly because it is a good story. It is fascinating for another reason as well. It raises a serious issue about the role that technology should play in the world.

This question is hinted at in the full title of Shelley's book: *Frankenstein: Or, the Modern Prometheus.* Prometheus was one of the gods of ancient Greece. According to legend, he created humans from clay. He also stole fire and gave it to the world. These acts defied Zeus, the chief god. Zeus punished Prometheus by torturing him every day for all eternity.

Shelley used Prometheus in her book's title because she felt that technology can be dangerous—

that it can be used for both good and evil. For example, fire is useful for warmth and cooking, but it can also destroy cities and kill people. Shelley's character, Dr. Frankenstein, hoped to conquer death and disease by creating artificial life. However, his work went horribly wrong, and his invention became an uncontrollable monster.

JOLTING THE FROG

Dr. Frankenstein's dangerous experiments were part of what today are called the **life sciences**. These sciences are the study of living things. Together they form many related branches of medicine and biology.

Doctors and researchers in Shelley's time did not completely understand how the human body

Dr. Frankenstein switches on a machine that sends electric current through his monster's body and brings it to life.

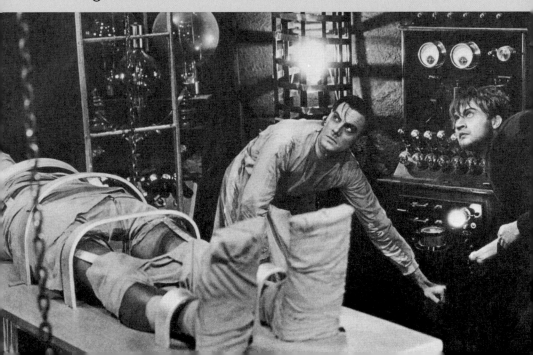

Italian biologist Luigi Galvani and his team apply jolts of electricity to the legs of a frog.

worked, or what created life. These topics were fascinating to them, however, and scientists conducted many experiments to try to understand their mysteries. The scientists were especially interested in exploring the boundary between life and death. Like Dr. Frankenstein, they wanted to know how to cure disease or even discover the key to life. Many people of the time objected to these experiments, however. They felt that it was wrong to "play God" by tampering with nature.

Scientists and doctors in Shelley's time made many breakthroughs, and they formed many theories. For example, in the late 1700s an Italian biologist named Luigi Galvani discovered that the legs of a dead frog jumped when given a jolt of electricity. (Electricity was a newly discovered thing in those

Frankenstein

days.) Galvani found that the frog's legs jumped even if they were no longer attached to its body. The scientist did not understand why this happened, but he suspected that it was caused by animal electricity, which is what he called the life force of the frog.

Such experiments led to attempts to revive people who had recently died. Some scientists jolted dead bodies with electricity. Others tried combinations of chemicals. All these experiments were unsuccessful. However, Shelley surely had such experiments in mind when she made up the story of Dr. Frankenstein.

ROBBING GRAVES

Another important part of the Frankenstein story concerns the practice of grave robbing. This was something else that Shelley borrowed from real life. Medical researchers needed a steady supply of fresh human bodies in order to continue their experiments. Medical schools also needed a steady supply of these **cadavers** in order to teach students about such topics as anatomy.

Unfortunately, there were never enough cadavers to go around. Medical students and researchers could not use just any body from a grave. For one thing, a badly decomposed body was useless. Also, most people were horrified by the idea of disturbing a grave. As a result, there were strict laws about cadavers. In England, for example, it was legal to **dissect** only recently executed criminals.

Frankenstein and Science 25

Because there was always a shortage of dead bodies, there was also a lively illegal trade in buying and selling them. Grave robbing was therefore not something that Shelley invented for her story—it happened in real life! Grave robbers were scorned by most of society as low criminals, but they were fairly common then. Sometimes criminals even murdered healthy people in order to sell bodies to medical schools.

"Now I Know How It Feels to Be God!"

More than 100 years after Shelley wrote her story, Universal made its film version. Movie audiences of the 1930s were still interested in many of the same topics as the original audience for *Frankenstein* was. They were still horrified by ghoulish grave robbers and terrified by creepy monsters. They were also still amazed by the wonders of new medical technology.

Furthermore, they were still fascinated by the idea of "playing God" and tampering with nature. The idea that people might be able to create artificial life was both dangerous and thrilling. In the movie, Dr. Frankenstein is excited when he succeeds in creating his monster, and he shouts: "Now I know how it feels to be God!"[4]

Today, people are still amazed and frightened by the same topics. For example, new breakthroughs in medical technology are helping doctors extend life, or at least improve it. This includes creating new body parts, just like those for Frankenstein's monster.

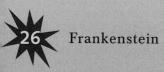

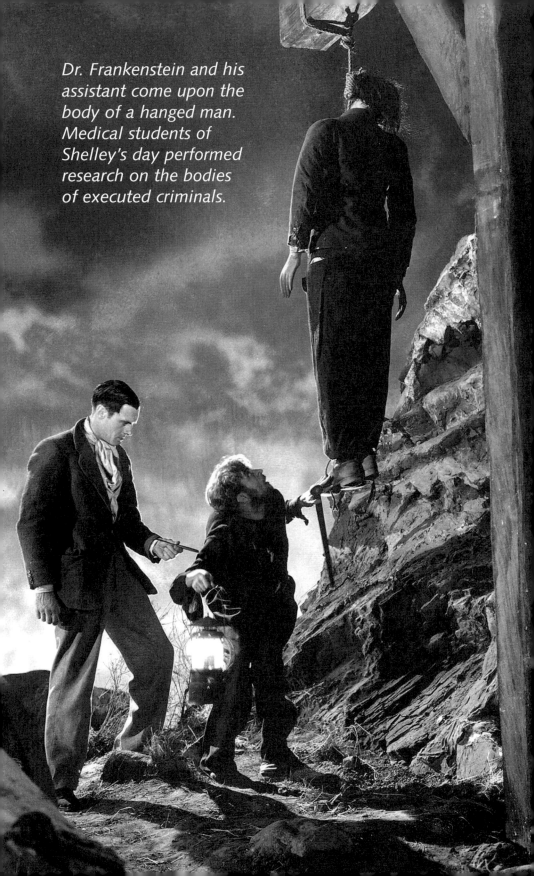

Dr. Frankenstein and his assistant come upon the body of a hanged man. Medical students of Shelley's day performed research on the bodies of executed criminals.

There have been many dramatic advances in **organ transplants** and **limb reattachment**. People can get new hands, hearts, lungs, livers, joints, blood vessels, skin, and other body parts. Sometimes these are artificial, sometimes they are transplanted from other people. For medical science, the possibilities seem almost endless. Maybe someday doctors actually will be able to give people new brains. (Maybe the scars will not be as ugly as the monster's!)

Scientists are also experimenting with ideas even more advanced than transplants. For example, some researchers are working on **cloning**. Cloning involves exactly reproducing an entire living creature, using information contained in that creature's **genetic material**. Other researchers are experimenting with **artificial intelligence**—that is, robots that are capable of thought, reason, and emotion. Someday these robots, like Dr. Frankenstein's monster, may come very close to imitating real human life.

A Great Benefit?

There is no doubt that medical advances have led to great benefits. For instance, organ transplants and new limbs people allow to live longer, fuller, and better lives. However, some people worry that there is also a dark side to this technology.

For example, there is a great demand for healthy livers, hearts, and other organs. There are not enough

of these organs to supply all the people who need them. This has created a **black market**, in which criminals illegally buy and sell human body parts. Some critics think this black market could lead to a kind of modern version of grave robbing, in which people are forced to give up their organs against their wishes. Some critics even worry that someday humans will be specially bred just so their organs can be taken for use in other people.

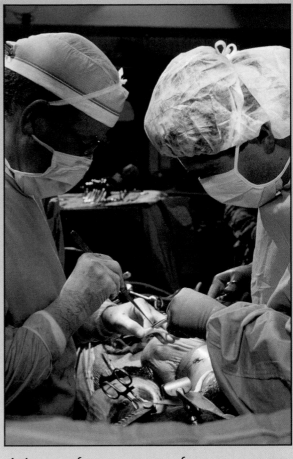

A team of surgeons performs an organ transplant, a procedure that was only imagined during Shelley's lifetime.

For the time being, such questions are just science fiction. It is important to remember that *Frankenstein* is just science fiction, too. Science fiction or not, Frankenstein's monster has become part of the world's culture. The creature has been in the public eye for hundreds of years. In other words, it is still alive!

CHAPTER 4

FRANKENSTEIN'S MONSTER LIVES ON

Frankenstein's monster can be seen in many places, but the best way is in the movies. The monster has made many film appearances since the 1931 classic that made him a star. Some have been good, some bad. Because the monster is still so popular, many of these movies are easily available on DVD or VHS.

After the original 1931 movie, the monster's next appearance was in a sequel that Universal Studios made. It was called *The Bride of Frankenstein*. Once again, Karloff starred, Whale directed, and Pierce did the makeup. Many horror fans think *The Bride of Frankenstein* is better than the original movie. They think it is scarier, with better acting and a more exciting story.

In this sequel, the monster has survived. He did not die in the first movie's windmill fire after all! He tracks down Dr. Frankenstein and forces him to create a female monster. This bride is a weird creation that has big hair and makes strange, catlike noises. An English actress, Elsa Lanchester, plays her. Lanchester also plays Shelley in the movie's **prologue**.

OTHER MOVIES

Universal Studios followed up with several more Frankenstein movies. They included *Son of Frankenstein, Ghost of Frankenstein, Frankenstein Meets the Wolf Man,* and *House of Frankenstein.* Most fans agree that they are good movies, but not as good as the first two.

A movie poster advertises The Bride of Frankenstein, *the 1935 sequel to the original film.*

One reason was that Karloff did not play the monster in these movies. The actors who replaced him did not have the same impact as Karloff.

There have been dozens of other Frankenstein movies over the years. Many were inexpensively made in other countries such as Mexico, Japan, and Italy. A British company, Hammer Studios, produced a well-known series in the 1950s, 60s, and 70s. This series included *The Curse of Frankenstein* and *The Revenge of Frankenstein*. The monster in these foreign-made movies does not always look like the familiar Karloff monster. The studios that made these movies did not have the right to re-create Pierce's famous makeup and costume.

Frankenstein's monster meets his bride in this scene from The Bride of Frankenstein, *a movie many people consider better than the original.*

Actors Gene Wilder (left) and Peter Boyle appear as Dr. Frankenstein's grandson and the monster in a scene from the 1974 comedy Young Frankenstein.

Sometimes movies about Frankenstein's monster were meant to be scary. In others, the role was played for laughs. One of these comedies is *Abbott and Costello Meet Frankenstein*, a 1948 film. In it the comedians Bud Abbott and Lou Costello play freight handlers who discover the remains of the monster and Dracula. They also meet the Wolf Man!

Another classic comedy with a Frankenstein theme is *Young Frankenstein*, a 1974 film starring Peter Boyle as the monster and Gene Wilder as Dr. Frankenstein's grandson. The grandson, a brilliant brain surgeon, re-creates his grandfather's experiments with funny results. This movie uses the same mad-scientist laboratory set that was created for the original film.

STILL MORE MOVIES

Over the years, some films have put Frankenstein's monster in unusual settings. One was *Frankenstein: The College Years*, in which two college students bring the monster back to life and try to pass him off as their surfer-dude friend. In *I Was a Teenage Frankenstein*, Dr. Frankenstein puts a teenager's brain into his monster, and the monster runs off chasing girls. In *Jesse James Meets Frankenstein's Daughter*, the monster's grandchild meets the famous robber in the Old West. In *Frankenstein Unbound*, the monster takes part in a time-travel experiment, in which a scientist from the future is sent back to Shelley's time.

Kenneth Branagh as Dr. Frankenstein holds Robert De Niro as the monster in a scene from the 1994 film Mary Shelley's Frankenstein.

Recently, the monster has been featured in movies with big budgets and spectacular special effects. For example, *Mary Shelley's Frankenstein*, which came out in 1994, is a serious film that stays fairly close to Shelley's original story. It has a cast of top actors including Robert De Niro as the monster and Kenneth Branagh as Dr. Frankenstein. Another example is the splashy 2004 adventure-fantasy movie *Van Helsing*. In this movie, the monster is part of a team of good creatures that do battle against the evil Count Dracula.

LOTS OF FRANKENSTEIN STUFF

One great place to find many different versions of the monster is in the world of Frankenstein **collectibles**. Horror fans keep up a lively trade in these collectibles. They buy and sell them in stores, at conventions, and on Internet trading sites.

Frankenstein collectibles like this painting are very popular with horror fans.

Some Frankenstein collectibles like this movie poster are worth a lot of money.

A Frankenstein collector can find all sorts of stuff in these places. Among the hundreds of different items are Frankenstein masks, makeup kits, toys, dolls, model kits, and action figures. There are also Frankenstein cards, stickers, candy and candy holders, cookie jars, bubble bath containers, puzzles, drinking glasses and mugs, posters, comic books, magazines, and even breakfast cereal. A collector could easily fill a whole house (or a castle) with Frankenstein stuff!

Sometimes a collectible can be very valuable. For instance, a huge, six-sheet poster showing Karloff menacing Mae Clarke is worth hundreds of thousands of dollars. Only one original of this poster is known to exist in good condition. Some collectors consider it the most valuable movie poster in the world.

Another example of a valuable collectible is a set of rare Valentine's Day Frankenstein stickers from the 1960s. When these were made, they were cheap items for kids to enjoy and then throw away.

However, like a lot of toys and collectibles, the stickers have become very valuable over time. It is rare to find a set in good, unused condition. A set in good condition can be worth $1,000 or more!

Stamps, Books, and TV Shows

The monster has popped up in many other places as well. For instance, he has been featured on two U.S. stamps. In 1997 the U.S. Post Office included him in its series of stamps about famous movie monsters. This stamp is a close-up of Karloff. In 2003 he appeared on a stamp again, this time as part of a series celebrating "American Filmmaking: Behind the Scenes." This stamp shows Pierce and an assistant applying makeup to Karloff.

Over the years, Frankenstein and his monster have been featured on posters like this one, stickers, and even postage stamps.

The character of Herman Munster from the 1960s TV show The Munsters *looked a lot like Frankenstein's monster.*

The monster is also a popular subject for books. As in many of his films, he is often shown in books as being funny, not scary. Some of these books are for kids, such as *Scooby-Doo and the Frankenstein Monster, Frankenstein Doesn't Slam Hockey Pucks,* and

Frankenstein Moved In on the Fourth Floor. Other books are for adults, such as *Dean Koontz's Frankenstein,* by the popular horror writer.

The monster regularly appears in many other places as well. For example, characters that looked a lot like the monster were central to two very popular TV shows of the 1960s. In *The Munsters,* it was the family's father, Herman Munster. In *The Addams Family*, it was the butler, Lurch. Also in the 1960s, Frankenstein Jr. was the hero of a cartoon series. He was not a living thing, but a 30-foot (9m) mechanical robot invented by a boy genius to fight crime.

HE LIVES ON

The story of Frankenstein's monster has remained popular for many years, and millions of people today know the monster well. Many things went into ensuring the monster's fame. First was Shelley's story, which introduced the monster nearly 200 years ago. Then came the 1931 movie, in which Karloff's acting, Whale's directing, and Pierce's makeup created the most famous image of the monster. Since then there have been the many other variations in movies, books, and collectibles.

Thanks to all of these, Dr. Frankenstein and his big creation will no doubt continue to live for a long, long time. The monster may sometimes be funny and sometimes scary. One thing is for sure— it's alive!

NOTES

CHAPTER 1: "IT'S ALIVE!"

1. Quoted in David J. Skal, *The Monster Show: A Cultural History of Horror*. New York: Norton, 1993, p. 135.

CHAPTER 2: THE MAKING OF *FRANKENSTEIN*

2. Quoted in Gregory William Mank, *It's Alive: The Classic Cinema Saga of Frankenstein*. San Diego: A.S. Barnes, 1981, p. 26.

3. Quoted in Skal, *The Monster Show: A Cultural History of Horror*, p. 132.

CHAPTER 3: FRANKENSTEIN AND SCIENCE

4. Quoted in Andreas Rohrmoser, "A Face for the Monster: The Universal Pictures Series: *Frankenstein* (1931)," in "Frankenstein," http://members.aon.at/frankenstein/frankenstein-universal.htm.

Glossary

abnormal: Not normal.

anatomy: The study of the human body.

artificial intelligence: A branch of computer science that involves the study of how to give machines intelligence like humans have.

black market: Illegal trade.

cadavers: Dead human bodies.

censored: Not allowed to speak freely. If a movie is censored, offensive parts are cut out.

cloning: A branch of science that copies living things by copying their genetic material.

collectibles: Things that are collected; sometimes they are valuable, but not always.

fiancée: Someone's future spouse.

dissect: To cut into pieces and expose the several parts (of an animal) for scientific examination.

genetic material: Information (such as height or eye color) that is contained in a living thing's cell structure and passed on from one generation to another.

life sciences: Any of several branches of science, such as biology and biomedicine, that focus on living things.

limb reattachment: An operation during which an arm or leg that has been severed is reattached.

mute: Unable to speak.

organ transplants: Surgery in which a doctor takes one organ, such as a heart or liver, from one person and puts it in another.

prologue: An introduction to a book or movie that occurs before the main story begins.

shooting schedule: The daily schedule for the shooting of a movie.

stage name: A name that an actor or musician sometimes uses instead of his or her real name.

surgery: Treating disease or injury with an operation.

FOR FURTHER EXPLORATION

BOOKS

Chris Mould (adaptation and illustration), *Franken-stein*. Oxford, UK: Oxford University Press, 1997. This retelling for kids of Mary Shelley's original classic is nicely illustrated.

Steve Parker, *In the Footsteps of Frankenstein*. Brookfield, CT: Copper Beech Books, 1995. This book summarizes Shelley's story and looks at the science behind it.

Ian Thorne, *Frankenstein*. New York: Crestwood House, 1977. This book uses text and still photos from the monster's most famous movies to briefly tell their stories.

WEB SITES

Frankenstein Castle - The Ultimate Frankenstein Film and Movie Site. (http://members.aon.at/frankenstein/frankenstein-start.htm). This site is a detailed source for information about the many Frankenstein movies, and it has some good still shots.

Frankenstein: Celluloid Monster (www.nlm.
nih.gov/hmd/frankenstein/frank_celluloid.html).
This Web site, part of a larger site maintained by
the National Library of Medicine, has some great
pictures of how Frankenstein's monster was
imagined in old plays and books.

**Frank's Reel Movie Reviews–Creature Feature
of the Month–Frankenstein (1931)** www.frank
sreelreviews.com/shorttakes/cf/cffrankenstein.
htm). A fan maintains this site, which has some
good stills, information, and trivia about the movie
and its sequels.

Universal Studios/Halloweenkids.com (www.
halloweenkids.com/k_games.htm). This Web site
has some Frankenstein-oriented games, including a
memory game and a puzzle.

The Woman Who Wrote Frankenstein (www.
suite101.com/article.cfm/history_for_children/
22800). A good article giving details about Mary
Shelley's life and work.

INDEX

PICTURE CREDITS

ABOUT THE AUTHOR

Adam Woog has written about 50 books for adults, young adults, and children. He lives in Seattle, Washington, with his wife and their daughter. He loves monster movies and has also written books for KidHaven Press about the Mummy and Godzilla.